This Tourism Logbook Belongs To:

____

____

Charleston, South Carolina is one of the most beautiful and storied cities in the United States. A popular backdrop for weddings, the Holy City has served as the setting for numerous movies and television shows.

Within the astounding array of historic attractions and historical markers, there are several buildings and tributes that honor or have served a role in African-American history. This tourism logbook is designed to help you organize and enjoy your visit to these sites.

After the name of the attraction, you will find one or more acronyms that indicate the site's official designation. These include:

NHL - National Historical Landmark
NR - National Register of Historic Places
SCHM - South Carolina Historical Marker

Generally, NHL or NR is used for landmarks or locations. SCHM indicates that there is a marker at the site. In this case, there may not be a building present.

A historical marker could also identify the place that something momentous occurred, such as the seizure of the Confederate vessel Planter by Robert Smalls, an enslaved harbor pilot during the Civil War.

Many of the attractions listed in this logbook are conveniently located in the Charleston Historic District. Notable exceptions include Drayton Hall and the Magnolia Place and Gardens, which are in the Ashley River Historic District.

In addition to carriage rides, there are many themed tours that will enable you to see the attractions with an knowledgeable tour guide.

Before you visit an attraction listed in this book book, use the page dedicated to the site to record important details, including available tours, accessibility and amenities.

An excellent resource for background information on the sites featured in this book is www.nationalregister.sc.gov. Click Charleston County on the map.

The book has space for telephone numbers, tour information and hours for actively managed locations. You can also record the date and your impression in the logbook.

While some attractions are open for tours conducted by the Charleston Historic Foundation, many buildings are closed to the public. You should determine whether the site is private or public. Please respect the property rights of the owners.

Table of Contents

Attractions in Charleston

Attractions in the Charleston Vicinity

Historic Attractions in Charleston

Aiken-Rhett House Slave Quarters (NR)
48 Elizabeth Street, Charleston, SC 29403

Cultural Significance: _________________________

____

____

____

Amenities (Nearby or Onsite): _________________

____

____

Website	
Private/Public	
Telephone	
Hours	
Tours	
Transportation	
Accessibility	

Nearby Attractions:______________________________

____

____

My Impression of Aiken-Rhett House Slave Quarters

Avery Institute (NR)
125 Bull Street, Charleston, SC 29424

Cultural Significance: _______________________________

____

____

Amenities (Nearby or Onsite): _______________________

____

____

Website	
Private/Public	
Telephone	
Hours	
Tours	
Transportation	
Accessibility	

Nearby Attractions:___________________________________

____

____

Date: ______________________

My Impression of Avery Institute

Burke High School (SCHM)
144 President Street, Charleston, SC 29403

Cultural Significance: ___________________________

____

____

Amenities (Nearby or Onsite): ___________________

____

____

Website	
Private/Public	
Telephone	
Hours	
Tours	
Transportation	
Accessibility	

Nearby Attractions:______________________________

____

____

Information on the Burke High School Historical Marker

Calvary Episcopal Church (SCHM)
104-106 Line Street, Charleston, SC 29403

Cultural Significance: _______________________

____

____

Amenities (Nearby or Onsite): _______________________

____

____

Website	
Private/Public	
Telephone	
Hours	
Tours	
Transportation	
Accessibility	

Nearby Attractions:_______________________

____

____

Date: _______________

Information on the Calvary Episcopal Church Historical Marker

Cannon Street Hospital (SCHM)
135 Cannon Street, Charleston, SC 29425

Cultural Significance: _______________________________

____

____

Amenities (Nearby or Onsite): _______________________

____

____

Website	
Private/Public	
Telephone	
Hours	
Tours	
Transportation	
Accessibility	

Nearby Attractions:____________________________

____

____

Information on the Cannon Street Hospital Historical Marker

Centenary United Methodist Church (NR)
60 Wentworth Street, Charleston, SC 29401

Cultural Significance: ___________________________

____

____

Amenities (Nearby or Onsite): ___________________

____

____

Website	
Private/Public	
Telephone	
Hours	
Tours	
Transportation	
Accessibility	

Nearby Attractions:___________________________

____

____

Date: ______________________

My Impression of Centenary United Methodist Church

Central Baptist Church (NR)
26 Radcliffe Street, Charleston, SC 29403

Cultural Significance: _______________________________

____

____

Amenities (Nearby or Onsite): _______________________

____

____

Website	
Private/Public	
Telephone	
Hours	
Tours	
Transportation	
Accessibility	

Nearby Attractions:__________________________________

____

____

Date: _______________________

My Impression of Central Baptist Church

Cigar Factory / "We Shall Overcome"
(SCHM) (NR)
701 E. Bay Street, Charleston, SC 29403

Cultural Significance: _______________________________

____

____

Amenities (Nearby or Onsite): _______________

____

____

Website	
Private/Public	
Telephone	
Hours	
Tours	
Transportation	
Accessibility	

Nearby Attractions:_________________________

____

____

Information on the Cigar Factory / "We Shall Overcome" Historical Marker

Denmark Vesey House (NHL)
56 Bull Street, Charleston, SC 29401

Cultural Significance: _______________________________

____

____

Amenities (Nearby or Onsite): _______________________

____

____

Website	
Private/Public	
Telephone	
Hours	
Tours	
Transportation	
Accessibility	

Nearby Attractions:___________________________________

____

____

Date: ______________________

My Impression of Denmark Vesey House

Emanuel A.M.E. Church (NR)
110 Calhoun Street, Charleston, SC 29401

Cultural Significance: _______________________________

____

____

____

Amenities (Nearby or Onsite): _______________________

____

____

Website	
Private/Public	
Telephone	
Hours	
Tours	
Transportation	
Accessibility	

Nearby Attractions:___________________________________

____

____

Date: _______________

My Impression of Emanuel A.M.E. Church

Harleston-Boags Funeral Home (NR)
121 Calhoun Street, Charleston, SC 29401

Cultural Significance: _______________________________

____

____

Amenities (Nearby or Onsite): _______________________

____

____

Website	
Private/Public	
Telephone	
Hours	
Tours	
Transportation	
Accessibility	

Nearby Attractions:_______________________________

____

____

My Impression of Harleston-Boags Funeral Home

Harmon Field / Cannon Street All-Stars (SCHM)
Near intersection of President Street and Fishburne Street, Charleston, SC 29403

Cultural Significance: _______________________________

____

____

Amenities (Nearby or Onsite): _______________________

____

____

Website	
Private/Public	
Telephone	
Hours	
Tours	
Transportation	
Accessibility	

Nearby Attractions:_________________________________

____

____

Information on the Harmon Field / Cannon Street All-Stars Historical Marker

Holy Trinity Reformed Episcopal Church (NR)
51 Bull Street, Charleston, SC 29401

Cultural Significance: _______________________________

____

____

Amenities (Nearby or Onsite): ________________________

____

____

Website	
Private/Public	
Telephone	
Hours	
Tours	
Transportation	
Accessibility	

Nearby Attractions:___________________________________

____

____

My Impression of Holy Trinity Reformed Episcopal Church

Richard Holloway Houses (NR)
221 Calhoun Street, 72 Pitt Street, 96 Smith Street, Charleston, SC 29401

Cultural Significance: _______________________________

____

____

____

Amenities (Nearby or Onsite): ___________________

____

____

Website	
Private/Public	
Telephone	
Hours	
Tours	
Transportation	
Accessibility	

Nearby Attractions:_____________________________

____

____

Date: _____________

My Impression of Richard Holloway Houses

Hospital Strike of 1969 (SCHM)
173 Ashley Avenue, Charleston, SC

Cultural Significance: _______________________________

____

____

____

Amenities (Nearby or Onsite): _________________

____

____

Website	
Private/Public	
Telephone	
Hours	
Tours	
Transportation	
Accessibility	

Nearby Attractions:_________________________

____

____

Date: _______________

Information on Hospital Strike of 1969
Historical Marker

Jonathan Jasper Wright Law Office (SCHM)
84 Queen Street, Charleston, SC 29401

Cultural Significance: _______________________

____

____

Amenities (Nearby or Onsite): _______________

____

____

Website	
Private/Public	
Telephone	
Hours	
Tours	
Transportation	
Accessibility	

Nearby Attractions:___________________________

____

____

Date: _______________

Information on Jonathan Jasper Wright Law Office Historical Marker

Kress Building / Civil Rights Sit-Ins (SCHM)
281 King Street, Charleston, SC 29401

Cultural Significance: _______________________________

____

____

____

Amenities (Nearby or Onsite): _______________________

____

____

Website	
Private/Public	
Telephone	
Hours	
Tours	
Transportation	
Accessibility	

Nearby Attractions:_________________________________

____

____

Information on Kress Building/
Civil Rights Sit-Ins Historical Marker

Mt. Zion A.M.E. Church (NR)
7 Glebe Street, Charleston, SC 29401

Cultural Significance: ___________________________

____

____

Amenities (Nearby or Onsite): ______________

____

____

Website	
Private/Public	
Telephone	
Hours	
Tours	
Transportation	
Accessibility	

Nearby Attractions:_______________________

____

____

My Impression of Mt. Zion A.M.E. Church

Old Bethel United Methodist Church (SCHM) (NR)
222 Calhoun Street, Charleston, SC 29401

Cultural Significance: _______________________________

____

____

____

Amenities (Nearby or Onsite): _______________________

____

____

Website	
Private/Public	
Telephone	
Hours	
Tours	
Transportation	
Accessibility	

Nearby Attractions:___________________________________

____

____

My Impression of Old Bethel
United Methodist Church & Information on
the Historical Marker

Old Marine Hospital / Jenkins Orphanage (NHL)
20 Franklin Street, Charleston, SC 29401

Cultural Significance: _______________________

____

____

Amenities (Nearby or Onsite): _______________

____

____

Website	
Private/Public	
Telephone	
Hours	
Tours	
Transportation	
Accessibility	

Nearby Attractions:_________________________

____

____

My Impression of Old Marine Hospital/Jenkins Orphanage

Old Plymouth Congregational Church (NR)
41-43 Pitt Street, Charleston, SC 29401

Cultural Significance: _______________________________

____

____

Amenities (Nearby or Onsite): ___________________

____

____

Website	
Private/Public	
Telephone	
Hours	
Tours	
Transportation	
Accessibility	

Nearby Attractions:_____________________________

____

____

Date: _______________________

My Impression of Old Plymouth Congregational Church

Old Plymouth Church /
Old Plymouth Parsonage (SCHM)
41 Pitt Street, Charleston, SC 29401

Cultural Significance: _______________________

____

____

____

Amenities (Nearby or Onsite): _______________

____

____

Website	
Private/Public	
Telephone	
Hours	
Tours	
Transportation	
Accessibility	

Nearby Attractions:_______________________

____

____

Date: ___________________

Information on the Plymouth Church / Plymouth Parsonage Historical Marker

John Schnierle Jr./Alonzo J. Ransier House (NR)
33 Pitt Street, Charleston, SC 29401

Cultural Significance: _______________________________

____

____

____

Amenities (Nearby or Onsite): _______________________

____

____

Website	
Private/Public	
Telephone	
Hours	
Tours	
Transportation	
Accessibility	

Nearby Attractions:_________________________________

____

____

Date: _______________

My Impression of John Schnierle Jr. / Alonzo J. Ransier House

James Simons Elementary School / Desegregation of Charleston Schools (SCHM)
741 King Street, Charleston, SC 29403

Cultural Significance: _______________________________

____

____

Amenities (Nearby or Onsite): _______________________

____

____

Website	
Private/Public	
Telephone	
Hours	
Tours	
Transportation	
Accessibility	

Nearby Attractions:___________________________________

____

____

Date: ______________________

Information on James Simons Elementary School / Desegregation of Charleston Schools Historical Marker

Old Slave Mart (NR)
6 Chalmers Street, Charleston, SC 29401

Cultural Significance: _______________________

____

____

____

Amenities (Nearby or Onsite): _______________

____

____

Website	
Private/Public	
Telephone	
Hours	
Tours	
Transportation	
Accessibility	

Nearby Attractions:_________________________

____

____

My Impression of the Old Slave Mart

The Parsonage/Miss Izard's School (SCHM)
5 and 7 President's Place, Charleston, SC 29403

Cultural Significance: _______________________________

____

____

Amenities (Nearby or Onsite): _________________________

____

____

Website	
Private/Public	
Telephone	
Hours	
Tours	
Transportation	
Accessibility	

Nearby Attractions:_________________________________

____

____

Information on The Parsonage/Miss Izard's School Historical Marker

St. Mark's Episcopal Church (NR)
16 Thomas Street, Charleston, SC 29403

Cultural Significance: _______________________

____

____

____

Amenities (Nearby or Onsite): _______________

____

____

Website	
Private/Public	
Telephone	
Hours	
Tours	
Transportation	
Accessibility	

Nearby Attractions:_________________________

____

____

Date: ____________________

My Impression of St. Mark's Episcopal Church

The Seizure of the Planter (SCHM)
40 E. Bay Street, Charleston, SC 29401

Cultural Significance: _________________________________

____

____

Amenities (Nearby or Onsite): _________________________

____

____

Website	
Private/Public	
Telephone	
Hours	
Tours	
Transportation	
Accessibility	

Nearby Attractions:_________________________________

____

____

Information on The Seizure of the Planter Historical Marker

U.S. Courthouse and Post Office /
Briggs v. Elliott (SCHM)
83 Broad Street, Charleston, SC 29401

Cultural Significance: _______________________________

____

____

Amenities (Nearby or Onsite): _______________________

____

____

Website	
Private/Public	
Telephone	
Hours	
Tours	
Transportation	
Accessibility	

Nearby Attractions:_________________________________

____

____

Information on U.S. Courthouse and Post Office / Briggs v. Elliott Historical Marker

Historic Attractions in the Vicinity of Charleston

Ashley River Historic District (NR)
Flanking the Ashley River & S.C. Highway 61, Charleston & Summerville

Cultural Significance: _______________________________

____

____

____

Amenities (Nearby or Onsite): _______________________

____

____

Website	
Private/Public	
Telephone	
Hours	
Tours	
Transportation	
Accessibility	

Nearby Attractions:__________________________________

____

____

Date: _______________

My Impression of Ashley River Historic District

Drayton Hall (NHL)
3380 Ashley River Road Charleston, SC 29414
(12.5 miles from Charleston city center)

Cultural Significance: _______________________________

____

____

____

Amenities (Nearby or Onsite): _______________________

____

____

Website	
Private/Public	
Telephone	
Hours	
Tours	
Transportation	
Accessibility	

Nearby Attractions:_______________________________

____

____

My Impression of Drayton Hall

King Cemetery (NR) Near U.S. Highway 17 & SR 19-38 intersection, Adams Run 29426
(28 miles from Charleston city center)

Cultural Significance: _______________________________

____

____

____

Amenities (Nearby or Onsite): _________________________

____

____

Website	
Private/Public	
Telephone	
Hours	
Tours	
Transportation	
Accessibility	

Nearby Attractions:_________________________________

____

____

Date: ______________________

My Impression of King Cemetery

Magnolia Place and Gardens (NR)
3550 Ashley River Road
(12.7 miles from Charleston city center)

Cultural Significance: _______________________________

____

____

____

Amenities (Nearby or Onsite): _______________________

____

____

Website	
Private/Public	
Telephone	
Hours	
Tours	
Transportation	
Accessibility	

Nearby Attractions:__________________________________

____

____

Date: ________________________

My Impression of Magnolia Place and Gardens

This logbook is one of the many useful resources created by the author to help you streamline and enjoy your life. Check out the planners, log books and guided prompts listed in Lynette Cullen's Amazon author page.